CONTENTS

ZOOMORPHICS AND POEMS.
By
Harry Bain.

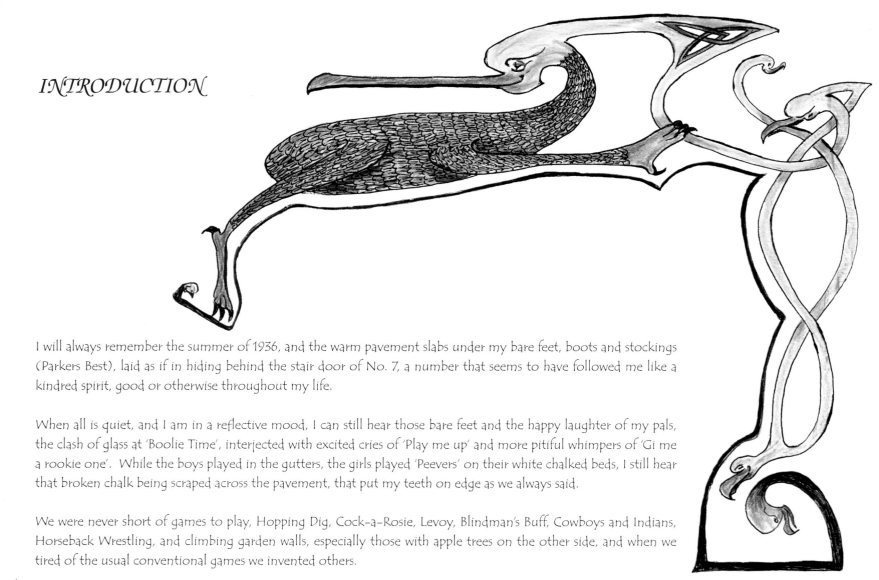

INTRODUCTION

I will always remember the summer of 1936, and the warm pavement slabs under my bare feet, boots and stockings (Parkers Best), laid as if in hiding behind the stair door of No. 7, a number that seems to have followed me like a kindred spirit, good or otherwise throughout my life.

When all is quiet, and I am in a reflective mood, I can still hear those bare feet and the happy laughter of my pals, the clash of glass at 'Boolie Time', interjected with excited cries of 'Play me up' and more pitiful whimpers of 'Gi me a rookie one'. While the boys played in the gutters, the girls played 'Peevers' on their white chalked beds, I still hear that broken chalk being scraped across the pavement, that put my teeth on edge as we always said.

We were never short of games to play, Hopping Dig, Cock-a-Rosie, Levoy, Blindman's Buff, Cowboys and Indians, Horseback Wrestling, and climbing garden walls, especially those with apple trees on the other side, and when we tired of the usual conventional games we invented others.

Our seasonal guider and barrow making, this was a ritual to see and relish, we would go and rummage around Assa Wass Scrap Merchants in Fountainbridge, for ball baring wheels for our guiders, and after many days of laborious sawing and nailing, carpeting, painting and finally the greasing of the axles, then we tested our very own Bluebird racing cars. One year I do remember, we had a race eight guiders, four barrows plus their passengers, we lined up at the top of Johnstone Terrace. I can't remember who won the race, but I do remember clenched fists from pedestrians on Grannie's Green side of the road, as we flew past at breath taking speed, and the anxious look on the face of the single decker bus driver, that will remain with me for all time.

Bonfire time came around as it did every year, with no more knowledge of Guy Fawkes than fly in the air. All that interested us was the accumulation of as many sofas, sideboards, chairs, and anything we could burn. We usually started collecting two weeks before hand, no earlier for fear of the dreaded, 'Wessie and Gressie' gangs, (West Port and Grassmarket) would steal our hoard from us. We guarded our prize possessions as if our very life depended on them, and many a cudgel battle was fought.

The only place suitable in those days for really big bonfires was the Canal Basin, this was situated where the Lothian House now stands. The Basin was drained in the early 1930's, which left a massive piece of waste ground littered with stones and debris of all sorts. This being an ideal refuge for rats, until the bonfires came, then they scampered out into the surrounding streets in every direction, running up-stairs, down basements, scaring the living daylights out of the adult population, especially the ladies, for some were as big as cats, but fierce and never to be cornered.

When they built the Lothian House and the Regal Picture house on the site of our Basin, it was the end of an era, but we were not put off. On the first year of our eviction we built a massive bonfire right in the middle of Grindlay Street, opposite number 7, all the neighbours were horrified at the sight of it. Barrow loads of bedding, boxes large and small, including Joe Croan's old fish boxes, that stank to the heavens, sideboards were dragged along the pavements, boys carrying floorboards, and bundles of newspapers. I helped to push a piano on rollers from Lothian Road, buy only got as far as the end of Grindlay Street, there it changed ownership for the princely sum of two shillings and sixpence. (twentysix pence) between three of us, spent on P. and B. (Pictures and buckies from the Main Point). We stacked the pile of wood assortments one thing on top of the other in a very professional way, for we were past masters at the game. Carpets, papers and smellie things to the bottom, big furniture around it, climbing on top of bits and stobs we pulled up more to make it higher.

Voices of excitement and laughter full of exuberance, bubbled out from the heart of the bonfire, mingled with screams and threats from all the women on both sides of the street, 'Get the police, call out the Brigade, ma' windaes'll breck'. Nothing deterred us from our ultimate goal, in spite of their out cries we lit the Boni', but unfortunately the Fire-Brigade, hoses at the ready arrived before the flames could reach the first landing of No. 7, on retrospect, just as well.

Every boy sooner or later tries his hand at fishing, but living in the centre of town the best I could do was 'Baggies' from the canal in Fountainbridge. A two pound jar with string tied round the neck, and a ha'penny net on a bamboo cane was the extent of my fishing tackle that was until one day, when the neighbours from the stair at No. 9, decided to move to another house after the death of their son, who continually banged his head on the outside wall, just to prove to the other boys he was tough. When the removal van was being loaded up, a few articles were still lying on the pavement, waiting for the men to stack them into the van, and amongst those bits and stobs was a Piebald Rocking Horse. I knew Willy had one although no one ever saw it, for Willy was never allowed pals in his house, but there it was, the living truth before my very eyes. I never saw anything like it's kind before; it was big and strong with a beautiful mane that shone like silk. One would think it had been brushed daily by a team of stable hands, real hair on the mane and likewise the tail, but what was most unusual for a rocking horse was the head, it was tipped over to one side as if to inspect the rider as they slipped their foot into the stirrup before they settled down on the well waxed saddle. Like the Highland Water horse in Scots folklore. I also was compelled to grab the reins of this particular 'Kelpie' and mount the steed. I jinked the Apaches arrows as I delivered mail for the Pony Express and rode cheek and jowl with Buck Jones, before realising my name was being called, for it was time for the removal men to take my horse off to another plain to graze in pastures new.

Willy's mother saw the look of disappointment on my face, she went into the van and brought out Willy's fishing line and thrust it into my hand, saying in a very sad voice, 'This was Willy's, he never caught a fish, only a drookin' when he fell in'. And with that she looked up at the window of the room where Willy died, letting out a very deep sigh, left in the removal van and returned no more. I used Willy's line often enough and caught some Mackerel, but who knows, maybe Willy tied them on.

Saturday afternoon at the Main Point was very busy, just to stand at the fishwife's corner to witness all the people coming and going, women with bag loads of messages, boys racing girds down Bread Street with dogs barking at their heels. Men blethering outside the Main Point Bar, waiting on opening time and building up a thirst you couldn't quench with a hosepipe. Children stood in a queue outside the Blue Halls picture house to see the Lone Ranger in some western saga, plus their favourite space serial, Flash Gordon's trip to Mars. But no matter whatever happened at the Main Point, one usually ended up with a plate full of mussels with plenty pepper, (I can taste them yet) and a bag of buckies with a pin, then off to join the queue for the pictures where I must confess the empty shells ended their doleful life's in the twopenny seats at the front.

The real street bonfires, gutter boolies, the making of bows and arrows, tight-rope walking from one dyke to another, (this did not please the ladies as we used their rolled up washing lines,) guiders, peeries, bully ten conkers, kick the can, ring a bell, tying door knobs, cudgel fights, telling ghost stories at the bottom of Burke and Hare's close, jousting with a boxing glove tied onto the end of a pole, and your balancing on home made stilts, or running a mile from the Vennel Methies, or the pipe smoking Ladies of the Grassmarket. These days have gone forever and only a memory remains.

These were the days of my youth, possibly no different from other children who have their own particular story to tell. Edinburgh has and always will have a special place in my heart, to roam the streets in my day was an adventure, but always safe.

The poetry I penned is about what happened in Edinburgh, and the Zoomorphic drawings are I hope, of a comic nature and different to the Celtic drawings I have used in my woodcarvings. Having embarked on this humorous book of humans taking the shape of Zoomorphics, I hope that in doing so cause no offence to the purists of Celtic Art. For one would be without a soul not to hold in high regard the works of our Pictish Artist-Craftsmen, who cut Pagan symbols like the Burghhead Bull, and in the early Christian era designed sculpture such as the Aberlemno Cross. One could go on singing the praises of the accuracy of the artists work in the Book of Kells and Lindisfarne, for no one will ever come up to their standard again.

Harry Bain.

ABOUT the AUTHOR

Edinburgh sculptor Harry Bain born on the 11th July 1928.
He joined the Royal Navy when he was 18, in search of adventure,
this he had for seven years, but that did not fulfil his ambition to see
more of the world. He made up his mind that one day, he would journey
to the far ends of the earth with his wife Catherine.

Harry left the Royal Navy in 1953, and enrolled in the Edinburgh College of Art.
He studied drawing and still life painting with Peploe, tried stone sculpture,
But found clay modelling with Norman Forest as his mentor more to his
liking, and after that studied wood sculpture in more detail with Forest.
His 50 years of wood sculpture has been described in his book called 'The Fire Within'.

Harry being a piper took a keen interest in bagpipe tune titles, this
gave rise to his first book titled, 'Bain's Directory of Bagpipe Tunes',
this led on to his second book 'Music, Castles An' A'.
He is currently working on a fiction called 'Pibroch for Duncan Ban',
and with all the world travel he has done with his wife Catherine,
makes good progress with yet another book entitled, 'Rockin' Chairs on Hold'.

Who knows to what realms his pen and gouge will take him next.

DEDICATED.

To

Mr. and MRS PLOOMIE

MUSIC, CASTLES AN'A'

MUSIC, CASTLES AN'A'

When maist folk gae tae Heaven, they usually find,
Angels playing harps, an' things o' that kind,
But I think o' castles, dotted a' ower,
And angels pipin' roun' the tower.

When I dee, nae hirst for me,
Jist whistle doon Zoomorphics three,
Bind them tae me, wi' ropes an' tassels,
An' let them flee tae yonner castles.

Shed nae tears for me, the moat is high,
The draw-brig' is doon in Tir-Nan-Og sky,
A happier sight ne'r ye saw,
Loved ones, surrounded, by Music, Castles an' a'.

THE CASTLE GUN AT ONE.

IS IT TRUE.

Is it true when sailors die, seagulls they become,
And people jump clean out their skins with the gun at one,
The Fishwife at the Main Point, has well and truly gone,
And folk no longer sup a mussel, coming from the pawn.

Is true there were sideboards, setties and manies a chair,
And cudgel fights with the West Port gang, from the close o' Burke an' Hare,
No more bonfires, no more cudgels, children no more hasten,
To play in safety without care, in one time Canal Basin.

Is it true dozing 'Peeries', no longer is the game,
Or 'Perverie Beds', in coloured chalk, will never be the same,
They've filled the holes in the causie stanes, for 'Boolie' time has gone,
Now it's T.V. Videos, Hi-Fi, Computers, and crumpets on the lawn.

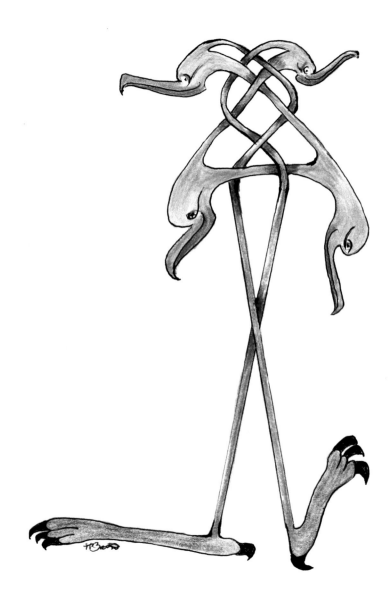

REV. THOMSON AT OLD EDINBURGH.

DUDDINGSTON LOCH

Farewell winter, I know it's not for long,
Snow and ice has melted, 'round the loch at Duddingston,
Curlers jolly at the 'Sheep Heid' quake
Talk of games, stanes and brooms they'll make.

Oh! it's hard to think on a winters night, when all around is dreary,
Lived a settlement of kindly folk, around the Wells o'Wearie,
Fish swam plentiful in Duddingston Loch, and deer upon the hill,
With the wind set right on a winters night, their voices, hear them still.

Painter Reverand Thomson no more makes retreat,
To 'Old Edinburgh' by the lochside, where curlers stanes did keep,
For peace and thought he takes gods pardon,
To walk unseen, in the 'Magic Garden'.

MAN'S INHUMANITY TO MAN.

THE PENNY ROPE

A fortunate man is he, to lye on a bed of down,
No thought of weary Eider ducks, would cause his brow to frown,
No care for the man when he closes his eyes, sleeps deep in quilt,
No thought for the man on the penny rope, asleep he has no guilt.

CEMETARY AT RESTALRIG.

SAINT TRIDUANA'S WELL

There stands at Restalrig, a well,
Where Pilgrims came by road and rail,
To kneel and pray beneath the skies,
Trid, Trid, heal our eyes.

Let the waters of the well, far below,
Once again in Restalrig flow,
Saintly lady, be our Bethlehem Star,
Heal your Pilgrims near and far.

A King to you his heart he lost,
A virginal deed your beauty cost,
Your blood had stained the hawthorn tree,
You sacrificed your eyes, that others may see.

ST. TRIDUANA'S CHAPEL RESTALRIG

THE KING'S CHAPEL OF THE COLLEGIATE CHURCH AT RESTALRIG WAS BUILT BETWEEN THE YEARS 1460-77 BY JAMES III TO A UNIQUE DESIGN, HEXAGONAL IN PLAN WITH TWO VAULTED STOREYS. THE UPPER CHAPEL WAS DESTROYED IN 1560.
THIS IS THE LOWER CHAPEL, DEDICATED TO ST. TRIDUANA, WHOSE SHRINE AT RESTALRIG HAD FOR LONG BEEN A PLACE OF PILGRIMAGE FOR THOSE AFFLICTED WITH DISEASES OF THE EYE.

THIS MONUMENT IS IN THE CARE OF THE SECRETARY OF STATE FOR SCOTLAND. IT IS AN OFFENCE TO INJURE OR DEFACE IT.

LADY ON THE VENNEL STAIRS.

GRASSMARKET LADIES.

Where Grassmarket meets the Westport, on Vennel stairs so cold,
Sat old ladies smoking 'Cutties' witches, we were told,
When we passed they tried to grab us, no harm, I'm sure they meant
But slipped through their hands, like leather, knarled and bent.

As they sat with pipe and 'baccie', and their cup of instant cheer,
Forgive me in my innocence, if I stopped to lear,
Knowing little of their hardships, for they had more than few,
The Grassmarket Ladies, and the Methies' too.

THE PIPES YOU HEAR, WHEN YOUR EAR IS TO THE GROUND.

CASTLE O' CLOUTS.

A tunnel from the Palace to the Castle o' Clouts was made,
A piper marched from either end, and a merry tune they played,
Their chanters stopped, and then their drones, before they ever met,
Rats, like cats, their mid-day meal, the pipers, they had ate.

Search parties rallied at either end, ropes tied round their waists,
'Save the pipers'! A shrill voice cried, 'For pity sake make haste';
The parties moved into the tunnel, lanterns held high to their hats,
Their lights went out, ropes went slack, they, like the pipers, were eaten by rats.

They closed the Palace entrance, and St. Leonard's one as well,
Now who believes this awesome tale, that I so solemnly tell,
No trace, no evidence, can anywhere be found,
But on a certain date, the pipes you hear, when your ear is to the ground.

THE PIPES ON SINAI MOUNT.

THE BALMWELL

An early morning climb over ice clad rocks, and gulleys like a fount,
A tune was played on Scotland's pipes, on top of Sinai Mount,
Where God gave unto Moses, Ten Commandments at that place,
And Catherine charged by Scotland's Margaret, an errand full of Grace.

Catherine brought with her own hands, a flask of Sinai oil,
She dropped a spot by accident, on Scotland's worthy soil,
Oh! Scotland, Oh! Liberton, a lucky day for you,
Thank Catherine, a Saint, a Balmwell did ensue.

From out the soil where Catherine stood, this miraculous oil did ooze,
This Balm medication, to heal their parts, the pilgrims they did choose,
King James the sixth, gave royal command, a proper shrine to make,
With steps of stone, and easy access, for the pilgrims sake.

Bad tidings in Scotland, around about the time,
When Cromwell with his vandal ways, abused the Balmwell shrine,
No pilgrims now do we see, on tranquil sanctified ground,
But the Balmwell stands, as did before, with oil to be found.

HARD TIMES.

THE BEGGARMAN.

Frae the castle wa' the Beggarman trudged, an' causies shone black wi' rain,
He passed the building on the right, whaur cannonba' lodged in stane,
Nae Edina view, or crust of bread, was sought frae Camera Obscura,
Changed days Mr Beggarman, changed indeed, buckets now are fewer.

Walk on auld man your hardships lasts, happier times ye've seen,
Whaur also trod that Royal Mile, Mary Stuart our Queen,
On Lawnmarket wa's the ricochet sound, of music frae fiddler's bow,
Whaur Ceilidh folk danced, in the Beggarman's dream, tae reels by Skinner and Gow

HARRY'S HAUL AT GRANTON HARBOUR.

THE BIG FISHERMAN.

Oft' as a boy with worm and line, to Granton Pier I'd wander,
To try my hand as a fisherman, for fish like Mackerel and Flounder,
It happened a Mackerel, on my amateurs line was caught,
Then home to Mother to boast my wares, big fisherman, great Scot.

As it happened the fishing stopped, I was no longer a boy,
I stowed away my hook and line, and gave up play for ploy,
No more hooks, no more line, from reels on waters laid,
The only reels that I then used, was that on the bag-pipes played.

The years roll by and I get older, but thoughts of fishing still return,
Thoughts like, bare foot boys catching 'Baggies', in the Blackford burn,
Or bringing out a Rainbow Trout, from deep and tranquil Lochs,
And beach-casting, far out to sea, from Tantallon Rocks.

GOOSE STEPS ON THE STAIRS.

A PUPPET'S REQUEST

I am just a puppet, and my maker pulls my strings,
Not like you, my arms of wood, you have feathery wings,
They all laughed and smiled at me, when my paint was fresh,
Now I'm chipped, and very old, I'm really quite a mess.

My feathery friend it's plain to see,
Upon my bed you startled me,
Do you still step on Bowersha' stairs?
Or are you but a ghost of yester-year.

I dream of goose-steps, on the stair,
Of paraffin and wax, that permeate the air,
I beg you, with your wings so strong and soft,
Take me; fly me, to our maker in the loft.

ANGUS BY HIS TREE.

THE ANGUS TREE.

Will you walk your dogs awhile with me,
To yonder hill and the Angus tree,
Where pastoral scenes like, rider and horse,
Blends with Blackfords bright with gorse.

See Edina's skyline, our treasured land,
From Firth of Forth, to Gullane Sand,
Oh! Scotland, at least this day we're free,
To sit ablow the Angus Tree.

Through the world's window, we've seen many sights,
From Jaffa Gate, to the Andean Heights,
No happier sight was made for me,
You, and your dogs, 'round the Angus Tree.

ABLUTIONS.

THE BATH-HOUSE.

For architects and masons to build a house so quaint,
To make historians pen their way, and artists they did paint,
Could you imagine royal servants, a bath for Mary fill?
Or Mary Stuart, Scotland's Queen, to bathe at Abbeyhill? .

This silly talk of bath-house, on my deaf ears does fall,
Could not a Queen command a bath, within the palace wall? ,
Think not of bathing, or house of stone, but think you this instead,
How those who plotted against our Queen, and how she lost her head.

WELLS O' WEARIE.

COMPARSIONS.

Parched I've been and my thoughts returned,
To the wells o' Edinburgh Toon,
Where people supped and filled a flask,
On a Sunday afternoon,
As boys we played on the Castle Rock,
With cheeks glowing pink,
In King's stable trough, we slaked our thirst,
Where horses stopped to drink.

Children longed for snowy days, and on the Pentlands near,
Fancy hats, toboggans, and all the skiing gear,
There was no need for us to wait, until the snow was seen,
Our Mother's shovel we did take, to sledge in 'Grannie's Green'.

SLEDGING IN GRANNIE'S GREEN.

COMPARSIONS.

Birthday parties with trampolines, cakes and cokes galore,
Not like the 'spring' we jumped on, outside Parker's store,
Now it's daddy drive me to the school, and mummy bring me back,
For us on lorry's, we did 'Cantor', no transport did we lack.

Trannies---T.Vs---Pop and gigs,
No blindman's buff, or hopping digs,
Bring back the boys that climbed dykes three,
To steal an apple from the Minister's tree.

CRAIGMILLAR DOORWAY TO KEEP

THE CASTLE GHOST.

THE CASTLE GHOST.

I've walked through the archway in a reverent way,
Thought I saw Mary kneel to pray,
Rubbed my hands across the stane,
Sure that Bothwell did the same.

A trickle of water, a mildew smell,
Listened to the walls, a story to tell,
Go back stranger, walk not this way,
For this is my castle, forever, and a day.

SEAN McVEY'S ABODE.

Once a pipeband full of pride marched down the Blackford Glen,
One woman, smartly dressed, and of course twelve men,
Ra, ta, tat,...ra, ta, tat, the drummers played, not unlike Morse code,
Chests out, and heading west, for Sean McVeys's abode.

March, march, the 'Cameron Men', the pipers they played true,
And following that, and just as smart, the 'Pibroch O'Donul Dhu',
Fingers tingled, that Remembrance Day, whilst marching down the
road,
Plaids were flying in the icy breeze, near Sean McVey's abode.

Take it easy and watch your step, that was Pipie's retort,
Remember the mascot, young McVey, his legs are very short,
Big Tam banged his drum much softer, as if to ease his load,
And made the marching easier, to Sean McVey's abode.

SEAN McVEY'S ABODE.

Pipers in step to the 'Drummer's Call', and through Sean's ornate gate,
All the men were six foot tall, including piper Kate,
My praise and honour to this band, I give in humble ode,
This gallant group that marched that day, to Sean McVey's abode.

We marched right up to Sean's front door, with 'Barren Rocks of Aden',
And there in view a feast for Kings, the tables they were laden,
Pies, cheeses and plenty more, this is their usual mode,
To welcome friends with open arms, at Sean McVey's abode.

HAPPY SOAPER.

SOAPERS STOOL.

Where Morrison St. met Newport St., a Barber's shop stood there,
For shaving grumpy grizzly beards, and cutting of the hair,
Outside there was a spiral pole, hand painted red and white,
Window glass, washed and polished, always gleaming bright.

One day from school with books in hand, my running feet did tread,
Wide eyed I spied on the barber's window, a notice to be read,
I rubbed my eyes in disbelief, as the sweat ran down my chin,
'SMART BOY WANTED, MUST BE CLEAN, PLEASE APPLY WITHIN'.

The job I wanted, whatever it was, so off to a nearby stair,
I ran the only comb I had, four fingers through my hair,
As a boy I was smart enough, buy right then not so clean,
I closed my shirt and rubbed my boots, before I could be seen.

50

My clean up over, and through the shop door, I walked with hopeful care,
A moustachioed man with razor in hand, beckoned me sit on a chair,
'Please sir', I said, shifting my stance, 'I'm after the job on the glass',
Over spectacle rims he furtively looked, to see if I would pass.

A soap lathered customer sat in the chair, awaiting the masterly strokes,
While two boys waited for 'Short all over', and laughed at 'Comic Cut' jokes,
The barber asked, 'Does mother know', and added, 'I wasn't all that tidy'.
He pondered awhile and then remarked, 'You're small, but start on Friday.

I ran pel-mel to tell my mother, that fortunes come our way, and say,
My job on Saturday is 8 'till 7, and two hours every day,
Mother made a long white apron, that nearly went 'round twice.
A stool for me, a cabinetmaker, made for half the price.

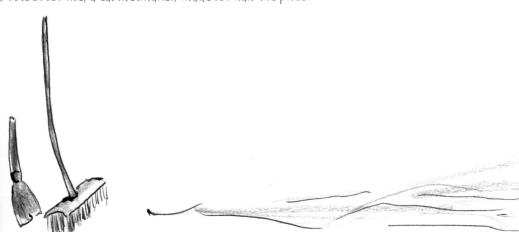

Into the shop with my 'Peaks' in, with stool and apron too,
I started work that Friday night, my duties more that few,
To sweeping floors and brushing coats, and sink cleaning in that place,
And hot towels wrapped around the head, and soaping of the face.

A happy soaper I had been, soaping many a bristled chin,
I'd soap a happy fattie face, and sometimes grumpy thin,
For washing windows or washing heads, I'd do this after school,
But no way could I do my job, without my soaper's stool.

For two years I 'Erasmic' used, countless bars to fill a lorry
And swept up tons of clipped off hair, to fill the Blackford quarry,
My boss he said, 'On leaving school, stay and make a trade',
But outside life was just beginning, my fortune to be made,
I bade farewell to a kind employer, and four walls on the yule,
And he in turn did the same, to short legs, ----------and the stool.

THIS IS MY ORIGINAL STOOL

THE MILK GIRL.

I'm half awake; my dreams complete, my dream a pastoral scene,
Of Pansies with their smiling faces, and the lyrical blackbird song,
My bed is cosy but my clock ticks on, like the beating heart of life, unseen.
I hear those footsteps on the hall floor; I know I don't have long.

The voice in my dark-room beckons to me, and, it's no surprise,
Come on girl, get you up, you know it's time to RISE!!!,
I pull upon my slender frame; my clothes I feel are cold,
I hope and pray I won't do this when I'm grey and old.

Hot tea and fireside toast, alas, I can no longer tarry,
So through the dark and wintry snow to Redpath and my barrow,
Outside Redpath's dairy door, the barrows are lined up,
Pints and quarts to be delivered, for their morning cup.

Many's a day the snow was deep, and the barrow stuck hard fast,
I knew my dream of sunny days and Pansies wouldn't last,
To dig around those massive wheels, my hands were like to drop,
St. Christopher, where are you? For you're my only hope.

Young folk did, what they wouldn't do now,
Fill milk bottles from the cow,
For those days you took your turn,
To scoop and fill, straight from the churn.

PERFORMERS.

Saturday night and the town is busy, and shop lights flood the street,
Work for most is over and done, all spruced up and friends to meet,
Where's my tie? Is that my shirt? And Oh! Did I polish my shoes?
Do you think there'll be a queue at the Rutland, hurry, hurry, no time to lose.

Older brothers dressed to kill, off they go and I'm alone, well, not quite,
For out the house and down the banister, ten steps at a time, so bright,
I venture out into the night, with alacrity, but silent, closing the stair door behind,
I am alone but not for long, the 'Grindlay Gang' I'll find.

'Ah! Gus, you're here already', when does the show begin?
'The man wi' yin leg, he's at the corner, he's about tae sing'
'Does he hae his dog, the yin that barks?, I hae a bone for him,
'Aye he's there, an' barkin' yet, wi' his nose well in the beggin' tin'.

'Look Gus, here's the tumblers, tae dae their balancing act,
That man's dae'n a cairtwheel, yin's taen a faw, ye think his heid is cracked?
'Nae fear o' it he's up an' awa', as if nowt ding I'm,…. But nae mair capers,
But look ye here, there's yon mannie, that makes wee lassies oot o' torn up papers.

One performance after another, singers, dancers, jugglers, and paper clippers too,
All did their best to entertain, the happy folk, in the Lyceum queue,
The street was empty, the Theatres were full, no need to shelter in Pagano's
So off back home to my silent room, where the flickering gaslight glows.

Sunday, ah! Sunday, a day of rest but not for Tony and his ice cream barrow,
He scoops out 'Skyscrapers' and 'King Kongs', as if there was no tomorrow,
In the late afternoon the fiddler played, then clip clop, clip clop Mrs. Dunlop came,
Donkey, barrel organ, music an' a', will forever remain in the hall of fame.

THE FLIGHT OF THE LAURISTON GHOSTS.

THE LAURISTON LAIRD.

The Lauriston Laird is guid an' braw,
An' his guid lady wife an' a',
The castle they've made new an' bricht,
Piper rest yer pipes the nicht.

In the India room, the lady waits,
Weary travellers, tae suffocate,
Piper clasp the ladies hand,
Pipe awa', tae anither land.

MOON SEARCHERS.

Mr and Mrs PLOOMIE

Like true Zoomorphics they're linked together,
Up Pressie Ave, in variable weather,
No fear of dark, or Man in Moonie,
The watchful Mr And Mrs Ploomie.

ALWAYS.

BOD-A-CHAN.

What after slumbers the mirror reflects, it isn't really you,
And all the things that you believe in never will come true,
The clock on the wall, with fretwork chipped, and hands stopped at three,
Bathe my eyes, my weary eyes, with the sight of thee.

I groped the sideboard, my spectacle case, to view my lonely room,
From an open drawer, a trick is played, a whiff of your perfume,
Why must I an old man, remain in day-dream torpor?
To hold and see, just in thoughts, but not to hold you proper.

I search the room in fumbled ways, for I am ageing fast,
A whisp of hair from a carpet ill kept, memento from the past,
I looked in a cupboard, and on a shelf, a pretty card that says,
A merry Christmas darling, I love you,………always.

LADY IN THE COWGATE.

AULD LANG SYNE.

Pardon me priest that I may see the face of my creator,
my kith and kin taken to his side,
Let me see with my own eyes, and not in dreams, the buildings
of old, the people Lang Syne gone to their rest,
Let me hear the happy laughter, the cry of the babe,
The running of feet, that has worn the Mason's stone.

For I have walked the Edinburgh Streets, Close and Pend,
In search of you that just remains a tale in the past,
Let us in joyous spirit the world over, clasp hands and
remain for all eternity,
One Celtic Triangle of friendship, just for Auld Lang Syne

ZOOMORPHICS WITHOUT POEMS.

The following Zoomorphics were drawn for my book called 'Music Castles Ghosts An'A',
The book consists of bagpipe tunes related to Castles, plus the story of the Castles and their ghosts, but anyone not interested in that particular type of book, may find the related drawings of the Zoomorphics of some interest. Therefore I take this opportunity to have them included in this book they are not of a serious nature, but hopefully they may bring a smile to the eyes of the beholder.

I have found in doing wood sculpture, that the intricate Celtic designs can be quite absorbing and fascinating, more especially if you make up your own designs.

I have included one or two wood sculptures to illustrate how Zoomorphics can be used, but there are many ways you can utilise them, for instance and apart from wood sculpture, painting, leatherwork, needlework, pyrography, silk screen printing, carpet making, just to mention a few ideas, the list is endless, and if you make up your own design on what ever particular art you choose to follow it will give more satisfaction so, may I take this opportunity to wish you well in your pursuit of 'Art for Arts sake'.

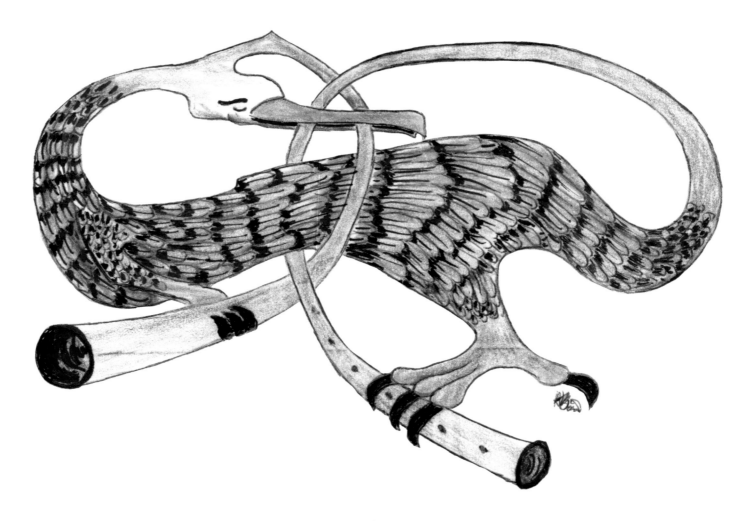

MOCHRUM.
In book Music, Castles, Ghosts An' A'.

FLOORS.
In book Music, Castles, Ghosts An' A'.

GARTH.
In book Music, Castles, Ghosts An' A'.

STALKER.
In book Music, Castles, Ghosts An' A'.

TAYMOUTH.
In book Music, Castles, Ghosts An' A'.

ERCHLESS.
In book Music, Castles, Ghosts An' A'.

BORVE.
In book Music, Castles, Ghosts An' A'.

AIRTH.
In book Music, Castles, Ghosts An' A'.

BORTHWICK.
In book Music, Castles, Ghosts An' A'.

ENCOURAGEMENT.
In book Music, Castles, Ghosts An' A'.

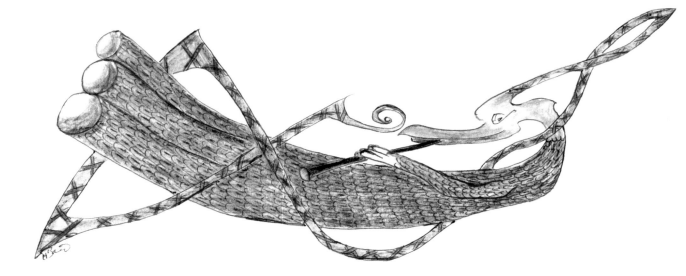

ABERGELDIE.

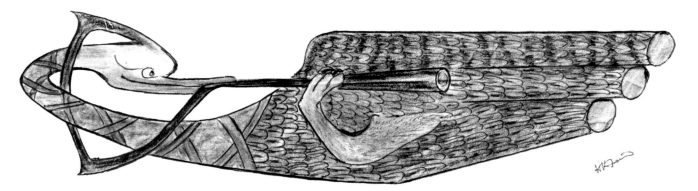

LOCHRANZA.
In book Music, Castles, Ghosts An' A'.

LUCKY McLEUCHER'S HOWFF.

One time Hotel in Minto Street, Edinburgh.

Wall Light:

Zoomorphics carved in Elmwood,
incorporating slab built ceramic boxes,
concealing electric lights.
Plus polished agate stones.

Ceramics and lapidary work by,
Artist Catherine Bain.

MANTLEPIECE in SCOTS.OAK

HOUSE SIGN IN SYCAMORE.
TWO ZOOMORPHIC BIRDS OF FRIENDSHIP.
TIR-NAN-OG: – (LAND OF THE EVER YOUNG)

MANTLEPIECE IN SCOTS.OAK

GLOSSARY.

H.B.

GLOSSARY ON POEMS.

(1)… MUSIC, CASTLES AN' A'.

This is the title of one of my books; it consists of bagpipe tunes, short stories of castles with a few Zoomorphics thrown in for good measure.

(2)… IS IT TRUE?

If you have ever walked along Princess Street at the stroke of one, you will if you are not expecting it, get the fright of your life when the one o' clock gun goes off.

The Main Point in Edinburgh was at one time the hub of the town, five roads converged at the Main Point, and the Fishwife carried her wares all the way from Musselburgh, and I'm sure her load was easier on her way home. The Canal Basin, where at one time, coal barges and other boats tied up and dropped their goods, the basin was filled in and the Lothian House was built, plus the Regal Picture House. The first film was 'Coconut Grove'.

(3)... DUDDINGSTON LOCH.

Duddingston Loch is situated in the Queen's Park, with Arthur Seat sitting squat like a guardian Lion, giving shelter from the cold north winds, this beautiful unspoiled corner of Edinburgh remains with the past, and only those who can walk where time stands still, will hear the happy laughter of the skaters on the ice, or the vigorous brushing of enthusiastic curlers clearing ice particles from the on-coming stones, for here truly in the 18th century, was the cradle of curling.

'Old Edinburgh' as referred to is the octagonal shaped building on the edge of the Loch, where curlers kept their stones and brooms, but was used later as a retreat for Rev, Thomson when he wanted to finish off a particular painting without being disturbed by any of his parishioners. If anyone called at the Manse, his wife or housekeeper would say, 'Mr Thomson is away down to old Edinburgh', so no lie was actually told.

The 'Magic Garden' does still exist, and is open to the public certain months of the year.

(4)... PENNY ROPE.

In the last century, in towns like London, Edinburgh and Glasgow, the 'Penny Rope' was so designed by owners of ill kept smelly rooms, for those unfortunates who could not afford a bed. A rope would be fastened at one end of the room, and pulled taught to the other side and tied in a slip-knot, when it was time to waken the 'Hangers On', a sharp tug on the slip-knot end, and down they all came... Man's inhumanity to man.

(5)... ST. TRIDUANA'S WELL

The tale of St Triduana is a bit sketchy regarding the loss of her sight, but it has been said that she was so beautiful, a King (again I know not who) was absolutely spellbound by her beauty he begged her to marry him, and would not take no for an answer. He pestered her so much that she could stand it no longer. One day the King came again to beg for her hand, but got more than he bargained for, on the lawn he saw Triduana standing with her back to him, and dangling by her side was the branch of a prickly thorn branch, and on the thorns – the beautiful eyes of Triduana. Needless to say the King troubled her no more. The story travelled far and wide about the great sacrifice she made, and before long pilgrims were arriving in train and coach loads from Glasgow.

(6)... GRASSMARKET LADIES.

At the bottom of the Vennel steps, the women all sat there smoking the half penny clay pipes 'Cutties' very cold and drafty in the winter, the reason for them being there was simple, they were put out from their boarding's, by those who ran the Women's Salvation Army Hostel, at the bottom of the West Port. Their lifespan would be very short indeed.

(7)…CASTLE O' CLOUTS.

In the early part of the 18th century, no man was better known in the Royal Mile than Gideon Murray of the Bowhead. Like many worthy citizens of Auld Reekie, (Edinburgh), Murray started in a very humble way in a little corner shop at the Bowhead, This shop was where Thomas Nelson, the publisher, subsequently began business. There Murray had his 'Claith shop' and along with his journeyman and three apprentices stitched and snipped from morning till night at the clothes to be worn by the Douce Burgesses and aristocracy of that period. A good craftsman, his business increased, and he became a wealthy man before reaching middle age. Then to the astonishment of his friends he retired to build a house in the country near to the quiet solitude of Arthur Seat. (Edinburgh's extinct volcano). All the land around St. Leonard's in those days could be procured at a comparatively low price. Gideon Murray was not the man to be discouraged by his acquaintances, who predicted that this would be his ruin. To live outside the Royal Mile, to them, was an unthinkable proposition. Ignoring the 'clash' of the Douce Burgesses in 1732 he began to build 'Mansion House' as he called it, and it was completed in two years. He placed over the doorway of his new home his own and his wife's initials, G and C.M with the head of an Eagle above a cornet, and the date.

This increased the bitterness that existed between the once humble tailor and those who openly declared that he was aping the gentry.

His wife, as proud a woman as Gideon, decided to have a great banquet to show off their new home. The invitations were duly sent out, but to the disgust of Gideon, who had hoped that one day he would be regarded as one of the leading citizens, and probably a future Lord Provost, only a few availed themselves of the opportunity.

Then some Bowhead wag christened the Mansion House the 'Castle o' Clouts' (cloths), as it remains today. The other Castle O' Clouts was situated at the head of St. Leonard's, which had no association with Gideon Murray's Mansion House. The whole tenement was built by the tailors' corporation in 1724, its Hostel was a favourite halting-place in the old coaching days to and from the South. Drovers too were frequent visitors, and the old tavern that survived until a few years ago was well known by the citizens, and sadly missed like a 'weel kent face'…once they go, they go forever.

(8)... THE BALMWELL.

For one night I had the chance to stay in St. Catherine's Monastery in Sinai, this journey has already been told in my book called 'Rockin' Chairs on Hold', but it was an experience I wouldn't have missed for the world. The journey through the Waddie to get to the Monastery, the bedding down in dormitories with mixed nationalities, men to one side and women to the other, the frugal food we were given and the cold we did endure, just to be wakened up at three in the morning to make the famous climb to the top of Mount Sinai, where it is reputed that Moses was given the ten commandments. I would never question that but I hope that when he went up it wasn't in the middle of December like we did, or try to play a set of Highland bagpipes, like I did.

It is also reputed that St. Catherine was charged by Queen Margaret of Scotland to bring back to Scotland a flask of Sinai oil. A drop of oil was supposedly dropped on Scotland's soil up at Liberton on the south side of Edinburgh, (at one time the name for Liberton was Leper Town, hence the 'Balmwell' from that time did come into existence, and remains so even up to the present day).
For anyone contemplating making the journey to St. Catherine's Monastery, I strongly advice you to do so in the summer months.

(9)… THE BEGGERMAN.

'Causie Stanes', were oblong in shape and were made of Aberdeen granite, at one time in Edinburgh all the roads were made of these stones. The Causie Stanes were especially helpful to the milk and coal horses. I remember seeing the latter trying to get to the top of Arthur Street with a heavy load of coal on the cart and ice packed snow on the road, at that time Arthur Street was reputed to be the steepest street in Britain.

'Cannon Ba' lodged in Stane'. Outside the castle, on Castlehill, is the Outlook Tower, whose Camera Obscura throws a birds-eye view of Edinburgh onto a table. Nearby is the Cannon Ball House, which has a cannon ball, embedded in the gable end of the house? Legend says it was fired at a couple of clansmen during the 1745 rebellion. Opposite it there is a Well that marks the spot where more than 300 women were burned to death for Witchcraft, between 1479 and 1722.

(10)… THE BIG FISHERMAN.

Granton Pier was a great place for boys and girls to go fishing, or just to look at the boats. I did bring home Mackerel once or twice, but you didn't need to be a great fisherman to do that, just drop your line over the side and pull up your catch, they were tastier in those days - no pollution.

(11)... A PUPPET'S REQUEST.

I was greatly impressed by my Uncle Philip, who lived at Bowershall by Dunfermline, and being a woodcarver myself, I do feel that I must have been indirectly influenced by him. My Grandmother's house in Bowershall was on it's own ground rented from some farmer for a nominal sum. It wouldn't be much, being there was no gas or electricity, just paraffin lamps and candles. The cooking was done on a large black range, liberally stoked with wood from the nearby trees across the river, where we had every day to draw our daily water supply in enamel buckets. There was this permanent smell of candle wax and wood smoke throughout the house, not unpleasant, but it was there impregnated into the timbers, on the walls and in the bedding.

I was billeted in the attic, one single bed with no light other than a stump of a candle, I also shared my room with boxes of old clothes, tightly wrapped newspapers, wood in all shapes and sizes, there was a bit of life up there also, I could hear them scurrying over the floor. But mainly there were puppets hanging from the rafters, puppets peeping out of boxes, dressed in sailor's suits, puppets sitting on puppet's knees, puppets dressed in crinoline, puppets hanging from the beams dressed in swallow-tailed coats, hung up like criminals, just for having a wooden head. When I put out the candle, all was dark and quiet. An occasional squeak, then the light would flicker in from the skylight and shine on the face of Long John Silver then I would get to thinking, maybe all his treasure is buried up here under that pile of newspapers. I wakened in the morning with the greatest fright of my life, it was a thud on my bed, and then a cackle and a flurry of feathers, staring me right in the face, practically nose to beak was this gigantic Goose, it wasn't in the least bit afraid of me, that's more than I could say about it, but on the floor was four more just as large and one sharing a box with a wooden baby with a broken arm and a sagging mouth.

In the morning I would go into my Uncle's workshop, and if you ever saw the film of Pinocchio and the old carver, this was it. Again hanging up, sitting down, puppets all shapes and sizes, dressed in uniforms, evening suits, ladies in flowing gowns, puppets finished, puppets in the making, the smell of hot glue, fresh paint, and newly sawn wood filled my nostrils, this is where I spent most of my time, helping my Uncle.

I made a visit to Bowershall a few years ago, I don't know what I expected, but I was to a great extent disappointed. It was not even a ruin, a few stones lay around the fountain but that was it, silent as the grave, no laughter, no gaggle of geese to cheer my day, no whisper from the ghost of yester-year, no winking puppet to welcome me home. The burn still runs at the back of the house, but lang syne washed away all the tales of Bowershall.

(12)… THE ANGUS TREE.

This unusual shaped tree is not unlike that of the Japanese Bonsai tree, and sits all alone on a hillock dodging golf balls on the Edinburgh Braid Hills golf course. It was here that my wife Catherine composed a tune for the bagpipes called 'Lament for Auld Angus' in remembrance of our old dog who died in his 20th year.

This poem came to me as I looked from our hotel bedroom window whilst on holiday with my wife at a place called Cusco in Peru, truly a lovely country, with very friendly people. It was on an Easter Sunday morning that I gazed over the courtyard and out to Cusco's narrow streets that seemed to converge to one focal point, a hill in the distance, which to me resembled a ridge on the Pentland Hills, at Hillend, near Edinburgh. Possibly, this made me think of home the Blackfords and the Angus Tree.

(13)…THE BATH- HOUSE

If you have ever been into the Palace of Holyrood, where Kings and Queens and other noble personage resided, you may think to yourself as I have done many times, and ask the same question, why did Mary Queen of Scots have to walk so far from that beautiful Palace across the lawns, to have a bath in poky little house in Abbeyhill? Admittedly, it is a quaint building, and to an artist's eye, well worth the painting. Maybe someone will contact me to provide facts about the Bath-House, but until then…

(14)… COMPARISONS.

Halcyon days, warm pavements, bare feet, truly happy memories. Down at Kings Stable Road all the carter's horses stopped for a drink at the trough, and so did we boys, before we carried on with the rest of our games and climbing the Castle rock.

Grannies Green, how the name ever came about I do not know, but it is the grassie ground that slopes up from the Grassmarket to the Castle. Words do have a way of getting changed over the years, but I walked down from the castle recently looked over the wall, and felt a great silence, no children playing there, where have they gone? No girls doing peavries, no skipping or the sound of their melodious voices singing.

> Eapnie teepnie, terry berry, ram tam toosh,
> Go to the cellar and catch a wee fat moose,
> Cut it up in slices, and fry it in the pan
> And don't forget the gravy for the wee fat man.

The only time I can remember getting together with the girls was when we had to help with the war effort, by having Spitfire Concerts in a backgreen in Spittal Street. I started calling it Spitfire Street, all the adults paid to get in, and all the proceeds went to buying Spitfires. I don't know how many we bought, but we had at least two concerts.

I never see children play as we did in days gone bye, where are they? the ba'stotters o' lang syne, they whae kicked the can doon Castle Terrace, or kicked the girls tin ower their beds o' chalk, or ran frae gangs up the Port, they'll a' be dae'n a jing-a-ring in Tir-Nan-Og nae doot.

(15)... THE CASTLE GHOST.

The Craigmillar Art Society for a number of years held a medieval banquet in the great hall of Criagmillar Castle, my wife and I were privileged to play our bagpipes at their functions.
Thoughts of Mary Queen of Scots, rushed into my head as I stood in her vaulted chamber. I rubbed my hand across the stones, knowing she probably did the same. This gave rise to my short poem of the Castle Ghost.

I took a photograph of my wife Catherine playing her pipes on the curtain wall, and it was just on the gloamin', I superimposed the photograph onto a photograph of Castle Menzie, to make the jacket of the first book of Music, Castles, An' A', to give a ghostly air about it.

(16)... SEAN MCVEY'S ABODE.

I wrote this poem to commemorate the march on Armistice Day 1985 of the Blackford Glen Pipe band; it was a cold bitter day but the hospitality was warm and friendly.

(17)...SOAPER'S STOOL

After the death of my father, I felt it my duty to take over the role of breadwinner, although only twelve years old at the time, I had a paper round in the mornings, which gave two shillings and sixpence per week, (26pence). I was offered a job in a Barber's shop after school and all day Saturday, when this great opportunity of untold wealth came my way. I realised another fifteen shillings, bring my total up to seventeen shillings a week, truly a King's ransom, well it did help at home. Although the hours were long it was interesting enough, but being small in stature I found it very difficult soaping the chins, so out of my first pay packet, my Mother had a stool made for me by a local cabinetmaker, which I am glad to say is still in my possession.

(18)... THE MILKGIRL.

Like most boys and girls liked the idea of having a job, apart from the soaping job I had my paper round in the early morning before school. I didn't like the winters with the dark nights and mornings, and snow was a great hazard, but grateful I was not to be delivering milk, for I used to see the girls pushing those heavy barrows filled with pints and quarts through the deep snow. My wife as a girl did just that, and found winter conditions the worst.

It is in looking back at certain hardships in life that makes you appreciate what you have and have worked for. I doubt very much if the young ones, would ever be allowed to do milk rounds as young as ten today.

(19)... PERFORMERS.

With only a wireless, that always needed attended to, such as batteries and accumulators, it's no wonder everyone went outside for their entertainment. Just to be out in the street was enough, it was safe to walk in the dark and most of the shops were open. Edinburgh entertainments were very good, if you had money to go, picture houses were in plentiful supply, the Pooles, Caley, Regal, Rutland, Tollcross, Kings, Blue Halls and the Coliseum, just to mention a few that were just a stones throw away from my house, and in my street I could boast not only the Great Usher Hall at the end of it, but also the Lyceum Theatre, where many a great artist past through the portals of the stage door. We would often stand waiting on actors coming out to get their autographs, hardly knowing one from the other, one particular actor came out and I asked for his autograph, he told me to come back tomorrow and he would have a signed photograph for me. I went back and he was as true as his word, I thanked him and ran home with my prize. The actor was Wally Patch a Londoner, maybe not that well known then, but in the London scene he was in a lot of plays and films, mainly black and white. I had collected a fair amount of autographs but never kept them, wish I had.

Outside the Lyceum Theatre there was always a queue, and picture houses as well, and where there was a queue you would find street performers, in all kinds of weather. We used to sit in the doorway of Pagano's music shop, just opposite the Lyceum and watch the acts. Some individuals would sing or do a dance, then afterwards go round with their hat or can. The can was the best begging bowl, it let people know he was coming down the queue. Some of the class acts outside the Lyceum were the jugglers, not only with balls and clubs but with chairs and people. One man would balance a slighter built man on his shoulders then toss him over to the other man waiting to catch him in his arms, the tension was electric in the audience queue. Some thought the show was better outside than inside. I saw this show one night and it was raining cats and dogs, the man who was supposed to catch the man in the air slipped before he could catch. The man in the air fell to the ground and landed flat on his back, the onlookers let out a gasp. The man on the ground jumped up as if nothing had happened, after their performance the crowd clapped and gave liberally to the collection… It's a pity you have to practically break you neck to get attention. Then, there was the man who used to arrive with a bundle of newspapers and start to tear them up, so we thought. He would fold them into squares, tear a bit off here and a bit off there, a bit in the middle, unfold the torn squares, and low and behold there would be a string of little girls holding hands. Sunday afternoon brought out the vendors in all shapes and forms, Tony the ice cream man, scooping out Skyscrapers, and King Kongs with plenty of raspberry. Mrs Dunlop would come up from the Grassmarket with her donkey pulling a barrel organ, and with the hot sun beating down on us, we would sit around whilst she gave a good selection of tunes. Happy, happy days.

(20)…THE LAURISTON LAIRD.

This Laird is the proud owner of two ghosts, one is a piper and the other is a lady. The former plays his pipes on wild and windy nights and is heard by everyone except the Laird, who will only hear it once, that is the night before he dies. The latter is a lady who has the bad habit of trying to deprive any sleeping guest of their breath, by putting her perfumed hand across their nose and mouth. Interesting castle…..Read, The Ghosts of Lauriston Castle, in my book titled, Music, Castles, Ghosts An' A'.

(21)… MR. AND MRS PLOOMIE

The weekly ritual on a Thursday night with Grannie's permission, brother and sister link arms and take their evening stroll to meet their Mother and Father at the bus stop, coming from their weekly film show.
The neighbours speak to them as they meander up the avenue, and chaff them on about hurrying home. For the Man in the Moon is looking at them, one friendly neighbour nicknamed them, Mr and Mrs Ploomie.
It seems like that the days of innocence are over, from an early age they are able to tell you, there is no Man in the Moon, there is no Santa Clause, there is no……what have they lost?

(22)…BOD-A-CHAN.

I am not alone when I say that getting old does depress most of us, no matter what you try to do to keep yourself occupied during the course of the day. Also people have a knack of reminding you, I personally try to forget it; I even don't like to see myself in the mirror. I constantly keep myself busy with one task after another, but no matter how hard you try, it creeps back into your thoughts, especially when you waken in the night. It was on such a night that the 'Black Dog' jumped on my back that gave rise to me writing such a sad poem, the last word 'Always' was our special tune.

(23)… AULD LANG SYNE.

We will never know how far sighted Robert Burns was when he penned his Auld Land Syne. Did he ever think that people the world over would clasp hand in friendship to sing his song? And if there is any life form on any remote planet, it wouldn't surprise me one little bit that they too are singing and having a right 'Gude Willy Waught'.

I stayed for a few days in New Otani Hotel in Tokyo whilst on a far eastern tour with my wife, A Japanese convention was just coming to a close when they all stood up, joined hands and started to sing in Japanese Auld Lang Syne. The same happened on the Island of Bali, we were sitting on cushions watching the floor show in our Hotel restaurant, a colourful display of young Balinese girls dancing to their own folk music. At the end of their performance the musicians started to play Auld Lang Syne, the girls came over to my wife and I, taking our hands pulled us over to the middle of the floor, where we found we were encircled by a mixed company of Nationalities. We were for that short period, friends of this beautiful world.

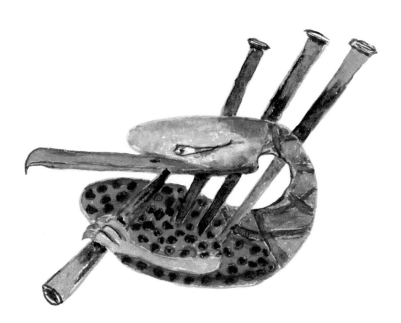

NOT REALLY THE END, ZOOMORPHICS ARE ETERNAL